Alexandra Stewart

Kitty Harris

WE DUG UP THE WORLD

Unearth Amazing
Archaeology Discoveries

Laurence King

INTRODUCTION

Hands up – who enjoys *digging?*

Whether it's at the beach, in a **garden**
or in a **playground sandbox**, most of us
enjoy a spot of *shoveling.*

Sometimes, it's fun to see
how far down you can dig.
But other times, you might be
hoping to find *buried treasure.*

Of course, it's pretty unlikely that you'll discover a
chest of coins and *twinkling gems* at your local park.
But I bet you've found other types of treasure.
Perhaps an old *toy car,* a *colorful shell,*
or a *rusty cent* from long ago.

In this book you will read about **real people**
who dug up some very *special treasure.*

In some stories, the diggers were invaders or visitors from overseas. And, although their precious discoveries **did not belong to them**, they still took them home! We now realize that this was **wrong**. That's why today some people are working for things to be **returned** to the countries where they were dug up.

But in each case, the items people uncovered had *incredible stories* to tell – about our planet and the people, animals and plants who have lived on it throughout its **long and extraordinary history.**

Let's meet these lucky people and learn what **amazing things** they *discovered* when they

dug up the

WORLD.

The ARCHAEOLOGIST'S TOOLKIT

There are three types of people whose job it is to dig.
The first is an *archaeologist* (pronounced ah-key-ol-uh-jist),
who studies ancient history through objects.

Here are some of the **tools** they rely on
to find their amazing *discoveries*:

shovels

picks

small ice picks
for finer digging

wheelbarrows

mechanical diggers

trowels

screwdrivers

plastic sheeting to cover
up digs when it rains

paintbrushes

lots of plastic buckets

wooden sieves

sugar scoops
for scooping up the dirt
and putting it into buckets

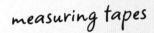

measuring tapes

toolboxes for small
tools like dental picks

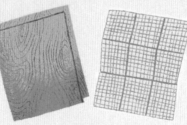
plywood boards
with graph paper
for drawing

cameras for recording
everything found

a video camera to
document what is found

balls of string and eight-inch
nails for setting up a grid system

The
PALAEONTOLOGIST'S
and GEOLOGIST'S
TOOLKIT

A *palaeontologist* (pronounced pale-ee-on-tol-uh-jist) studies ancient life through fossils and a *geologist* (pronounced gee-ol-uh-jist) studies the history of the Earth and what it's made of.

Here are some of the **tools** they rely on to find their amazing *discoveries*:

geological picks

geological hammer

hand scraper (useful for crags)

field lens –
to see tiny fossils

trowels and spades

rock chisels

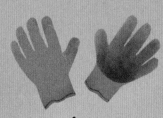
notebook and *pen*

tweezers – handy for picking up the smallest fossils

SAFETY EQUIPMENT*
*UNIVERSAL

goggles

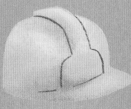
hard hat

gloves

first aid kit

5

We Dug Up a SEA MONSTER

When **Mary** and **Joseph Anning** went exploring at their local beach one day in *1811*, they dug up something **MONSTROUS** . . . the **fossilized skeleton** of a *massive sea creature!*

Joseph and Mary lived with their parents in *Lyme Regis*, on England's **Jurassic Coast** – an area famous for its spectacular *fossils*.

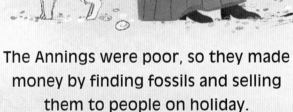

The Annings were poor, so they made money by finding fossils and selling them to people on holiday.

It was on one of these fossil-hunting expeditions that Joseph spotted the **strange-looking skull**.

When he excitedly showed it to his sister, she immediately set about **digging** . . .

and **digging** . . . and **digging!**

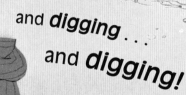

Several months later, Mary finally finished digging up the **17-feet-long** *skeleton*! The people of Lyme Regis were convinced that it belonged to a terrifying

SEA MONSTER!

As well as being a *whizz* at **finding fossils**, *Mary* was expert at **identifying** them too!

We now know that it was an *ichthyosaur* – an **extinct reptile** that lived in the sea around *200 million years ago.*

Mary continued fossil hunting with just her dog *Tray* for company. As the years went by, she made heaps of **GROUND-BREAKING** discoveries, including . . .

The first complete skeleton of the *long-necked Plesiosaurus* – also known as a **'sea dragon'**.

Another *ichthyosaur skeleton* – with fish bones from its last meal still inside it!

And the first known remains of a **'flying dragon'** or *Pterodactylus*.

Sadly, because Mary was **female** and **poor**, she did not receive the respect or recognition she deserved during her lifetime. Today, however, her scientific achievements are finally making the *SPLASH* they deserve.

Mary was so **brilliant** that **famous scientists** from far and wide visited her in her seaside home. Her work showed that the Earth was not a few thousand years old (as many people believed at that time) but **billions** of years old.

We Dug Up a DINOSAUR

12-year-old Nathan Hrushkin and his dad caused an uproar when they went hiking in the Alberta Badlands, Canada and stumbled across a *prehistoric* **dinosaur**.

Nathan had been visiting the area ever since he was little in the hope of finding his own dinosaur *fossil*.

He had searched **high** . . .

. . . and *low* . . .

. . . until one scorching summer's day in 2020, when his luck dramatically changed.

As he clambered up a hill, something caught his eye. Poking out of the ground were . . .

Millions of years ago, the Badlands National Park was a stomping ground for **many** different **species of dinosaurs**. These days they are a stomping ground for hikers and **palaeontologists**.

. . . four large bones.

With his heart thumping, he shouted for his dad to come and look.

Nathan **desperately** wanted to start digging, but he knew that disturbing the bones might **damage** them. So, he and his dad contacted a nearby dinosaur museum, which quickly sent a team of *palaeontologists* to investigate.

After months of digging . . .

and scraping . . .

and brushing . . .

. . . they realised that Nathan had discovered something very *rare*.

Nathan's hadrosaur is now in Alberta's *Royal Tyrrell Museum of Palaeontology*, but you can see other dinosaur fossils in museums all over the world!

These were fossilized bones of a young HADROSAUR that had lived 69 *million years ago*. What made Nathan's hadrosaur **SO special** was that very few dinosaur fossils from that period of Earth's history have **ever** been found.

We Dug Up An ASTEROID

In 2016, scientists found something **Earth-shattering**: tiny specks of the *asteroid* that wiped out the *dinosaurs*!

To understand their **cosmic** find we must travel back 66 *million* years, when an *asteroid* as big as Mount Everest **slammed** into the Earth at the speed of a **bullet!**

The force of the crash-landing was so **enormous** that the asteroid turned to *dust* and blocked out the Sun's rays.

Earth was plunged into a **winter** that lasted for many years – plants struggled to grow and animals had very little to eat.

The result was the **mass extinction** (death) of around *three quarters* of the Earth's species – including the *non-flying dinosaurs.*

It was not until 1980 that scientists came up with the *dinosaur-destroying asteroid* theory. They suspected a mysterious *112-mile-wide crater* on the edge of *Mexico* was where it had landed. But experts needed hard **evidence** to prove the crater had been made by the deadly

ASTEROID.

So, in *2016*, an international team of scientists drilled **almost a mile** down into the crater, through *millions of years* of Earth's history, collecting rock samples along the way.

When they studied the samples, they found high levels of *iridium*.

Iridium is a **rare metal** often found in *asteroids*.

The depth at which they found the iridium told them that it had arrived on Earth *66 million years* ago . . . the same time that the **dinosaurs** had been wiped out!

The **crater** stretched across the land and under the sea and was named the **Chicxulub** (pronounced cheek-shoe-lube) crater – after a town near its center. It is the **only well-preserved impact crater** on Earth linked to a **mass extinction.**

We Dug Up a
METEORITE

One winter's day, in 1920, a farmer called *Jacobus Brits* discovered something completely **out of this world** on his farm in *Hoba*, Namibia.

Tired from hunting, *Jacobus* was searching for somewhere to rest when he noticed a **strange** black rock.

Curious, Jacobus pulled out his penknife and scratched the surface. To his amazement, the rock *gleamed* like silver in the sunlight.

What on **Earth** could it be?

The rock was tough, but Jacobus managed to chip a bit away to take home to his wife, *Anna*.

Knowing they'd found something **special**, Jacobus and Anna took it to a rock expert (minerologist).

To their astonishment, he declared it to be a sliver of
METEORITE.

Meteorites are ancient pieces of other **planets**, **asteroids**, or **comets** that fall to Earth from space.

Back on the farm, an excited Anna began digging. After many days of hard shoveling . . . and a *lot* of huffing and puffing . . . she stood back to admire the meteorite.

It was **HUGE** – measuring ten feet long, ten feet wide and three feet high. It remains the **biggest** unbroken *meteorite* that has *ever* been found on Earth.

Scientists believe that the meteorite is around 4,500 million years old and was once the centre of an **asteroid**. It probably plummeted to Earth 80,000 years ago.

It is now one of *Namibia's* national monuments, so . . . if you ever happen to be passing . . . why not **drop** in?

It is mostly made of *iron* and weighs a staggering 67 *tons* (as heavy as around **ten male African elephants**)! That's why it remains where it crash-landed on Jacobus and Anna's farm!

We Dug Up LUCY

In 1974, two American scientists named *Don Johanson* and *Tom Gray* dug up a **3.2-million-year-old fossilized skeleton** in *Afar*, Ethiopia. Back then, it was the oldest human ancestor ever discovered and it **ape**-solutely transformed our understanding of human evolution.

The two men were *anthropologists* (people who study human beings) hunting for clues about how humans developed or **evolved** from a type of ape – a process that began around *7 million years ago* in Africa.

Don glimpsed part of an *arm bone* poking out of the earth . . .

Next to it were . . .

. . . *skull fragments* . . .

a piece of jaw . . .

and a *thigh bone.*

Bits of *skeleton* were **EVERYWHERE.**

When they pieced them all together, Don and Tom realised they had found almost half an entire skeleton of an *APE-LIKE* creature!

By carefully examining the bones, they gathered lots of important information about the creature.

They determined it was a *female* who had died when she was a **young adult.**

They could also tell that her brain was a **little bigger** than a *chimpanzee's* and **WAY smaller** than a *human* brain.

Lucy lives in the *National Museum of Ethiopia*, in **Addis Ababa**, where she is kept company by lots of fascinating *fossils* from around the country.

But the real **bone**-us was that they could see from the **shape of her skeleton** that, instead of walking on all-fours like an ape, she had walked upright on *two legs* like a human!

Up until that point, scientists believed the brains of humankind's ape ancestors had gradually evolved to become much bigger **before** they learned to walk on two feet. In fact, it was the **other way around!**

Although her scientific name is **Australopithecus afarensis**, Don and Tom nicknamed the fossil **Lucy** after the popular Beatles song *Lucy in the Sky with Diamonds*. But to the people of Ethiopia, she is affectionately known as '**Dinkinesh**' which means '**you are marvelous**'.

We Dug Up a POOP

Imagine searching for prehistoric artefacts and accidentally digging up ... a **POOP!** **YUCK!** Sounds gross, but Spanish archaeologist, Ainara Sistiaga, was **THRILLED** when she dug up some 50,000-year-old human dung at an ancient campsite in 2014.

The campsite, called *El Salt*, is near Spain's Mediterranean coast, and it was once used by early humans – known as **Neanderthals.**

Ainara made her discovery while looking for evidence of **prehistoric cooking** in the Neanderthal's *fire pit*. After examining rock samples dug up from the pit, she was surprised to discover they contained bits of *HUMAN WASTE.*

That's right! Some **naughty** Neanderthal had pooped on the fire . . . (although probably not while it was lit).

For Ainara, the ancient number two was a **number one find!** It is still officially the *oldest human poop* ever discovered.

The **poop** changed what historians believed about **Neanderthals' diets.** For many years, scientists were convinced that Neanderthals were **carnivores** that only ate **meat.** But this poop contained traces of **digested plants** – showing that its owner had eaten **veggies.**

If Ainara wins the prize for finding the world's oldest poop, the award for the **world's largest poop** goes to the *English city of York.*

Back in *1972,* archaeologists came across a **whopping** fossilized poop (known as a *coprolite*). It measured a **huge 8 inches** long and 2 inches wide and was probably the work of a *Viking.*

If you want to get to the bottom of this fascinating find, you can see the biggest poop for yourself at the *JORVIK Viking Centre* in **York.**

We Dug Up A
WOOLLY MAMMOTH

In *2010*, tusk hunters from *Yukagir* village found something especially **COOL** buried in icy ground on the edge of Siberia's *Laptev Sea* – it had orangey hair, leathery skin, and four big, **galumphing** feet.

So they began to dig . . .

and **dig** . . .

until they uncovered a *28,000*-year-old mammoth!

After its discovery, the mammoth was **preserved** for two years in a *'lednik'*, Yugakir's natural refridgerators.

Many internal organs and bones were missing, but its *skin, fur, brain,* and *muscles* were still there! They even found its *blood* vessels! It had been perfectly preserved or **'mummified'** by the snow.

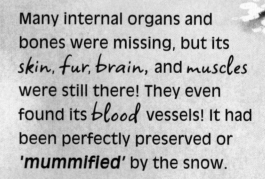

Although mammoths **died out** at the end of the last **Ice Age** (about **10,500** years ago), their **teeth, tusks,** and **bones** can still be found buried in the frozen ground. As the **climate heats up** and the **ice melts**, more remains are being discovered.

The MAMMOTH – nicknamed 'Yuka' (after where she was found) – was a **young female**. Bite and scratch wounds on her skin revealed that she had been **attacked** by wild animals – probably *lions!*

However, it also looked like Yuka's body had been attacked by **humans**.

This made scientists wonder if the hunters had watched the lions attack Yuka before chasing the big cats away and **stealing** the mammoth for themselves!

They also think the humans may have **reburied** the rest of the body in the frozen ground to keep it fresh for later. A bit like putting it in a *prehistoric fridge!*

Thanks to Yuka, scientists now understand more about **how humans hunted** in the **Ice Age!**

Scientists in *Japan* have been experimenting with Yuka's **DNA** to see if they can bring mammoths back from the dead!

We Dug Up a
BISON

On a hot summer's day in 1908, a terrible **thunderstorm** raged around the town of Folsom, New Mexico. When cowboy and former slave George McJunkin ventured outside afterwards to see how much damage it had caused, he saw something *incredi-BULL!*

Poking out from the bank of a creek were some **giant bison bones.**

George **loved** nature and learning about the world. Above all, he enjoyed collecting *rocks* and *fossils* that told him stories of the landscape around him.

He knew at once that the bones were *special.* No modern bison had bones that **huge.**

George dug a few out and carried them home to display on his mantelpiece.

Although he tried with all his might to persuade experts to look at his important find, **no one** bothered.

It was not until 1926, four years after George died, that two fossil experts named *Jesse Dade Figgins* and *Howard Cook* from the **Colorado Museum of Natural History** finally examined the bones and declared they belonged to an **extinct** BISON called *Bison antiquus*.

This, *plant-eating* **mega beast** had roamed *North Africa* during the **Ice Age!**

Excited by the news, archaeologists began **excavating** the site where George had made his discovery.

They hoped to find more skeletons to display at the museum. But what they actually unearthed was something with a much **bigger story** to tell . . .

On *August 29 1927*, they dug up a bison with a **stone spear point** buried in its ribs.

This was **GAME**-changing! Back then, experts believed humans had arrived in North America roughly **7,000 years** after *Bison antiquus* was extinct. However, this showed that they had got there much earlier . . . and had been living **alongside** Bison antiquus.

Although **George**, very sadly, never lived to see the amazing end to his story, it's **thanks to him** that **archaeologists** today know how far back in **history** they must go to tell the whole **story of humans in America.**

We Dug Up ANCIENT ART

In 1879, 8-year-old *Maria Sanz de Sautuola* and her father, *Marcelino*, explored a cave in **Altamira,** Spain, where Maria found something that would **re-draw** people's understanding of human history.

As Marcelino, who loved archaeology, carefully dug up the earth floor, a **curious** Maria wandered deeper into the **gloomy cave**.

Using a candle to light her way, she examined everything around her.

She was amazed to see a *painting* of a bull-like creature on the **rocky ceiling** of the cave. Except, it wasn't a bull. It was a *Steppe bison* – a species that had been **extinct** for many thousands of years.

The creature was *beautifully painted* with varied strokes and even engraving.

There were also paintings of . . .

wild boar, deer, horses, human hands, and curious symbols.

They reminded Marcelino of *Stone Age carvings* he'd seen at an archaeology exhibition in Paris. He realised that these paintings were also the work of Stone Age artists.

But when he shared his **amazing news**, professional archaeologists were **doubtful**. They didn't believe that Stone Age folk had the *skill* or the *imagination* to create such beautiful works of ART.

Some people accused *Marcelino* of being a **con artist** who had painted them himself!

It was not until *1902* – after the discovery of **more cave paintings** in *Spain* and *France* – that experts finally agreed Marcelino was **right!**

Stone Age people really had painted the pictures and they were clearly far more **advanced** than previously thought.

We now know that the paintings were created by **lots** of different **Stone Age artists** over a **20,000-year** period (between **35,000 BCE** and **15,000 BCE**).

We Dug Up a MUMMY

For years archaeologists had been searching *Egypt's Valley of the Kings* for the mummy of the ancient Egyptian pharaoh, *Tutankhamun*. But his whereabouts remained firmly **under wraps!**

That was until a rich Englishman called *Lord Carnarvon* agreed to pay a determined archaeologist named *Howard Carter* to search for the lost king.

After **five**

long

years,

Howard had found . . . **nothing** that would change history.

A frustrated Lord Carnarvon said he would only pay for **one more dig.** So, in *November 1922,* Howard and his team set to work for the last time.

Although **Tutankhamun** was only **king** for **ten years**, the discovery of his tomb made him the **most famous pharaoh** of all time! Thanks to King Tut, we know more about life and death in **ancient Egypt** than ever before.

After a few days, they uncovered . . .

. . . a set of 16 **secret steps,** leading down to a **blocked doorway.**

With the excited team behind him,
Howard opened the door to reveal . . .

. . . a passageway . . . leading to . . . another sealed door.

sigh!

Behind *that* door, they saw many *treasures,* including . . .

. . . *golden statues and jewelry* . . .

decorated *boxes* and *boats* . . .

royal chariots . . .

and a *golden throne.*

The most impressive discovery was the *sacred burial chamber.*
There, inside four **gold-covered shrines, a stone box,** and
three coffins (one made from solid gold), was

Tutankhamun's MUMMIFIED body.

It took the team **ten years** to record and remove the *5,398 objects* in Tutankhamun's tomb.

Alongside amazing treasures were everyday items, including bread,
meat, and even **fresh underwear!** Everything in the tomb had
been put there to help the King with his journey into the *afterlife.*

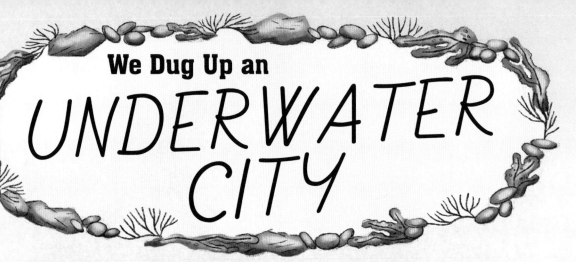

We Dug Up an UNDERWATER CITY

In the *1900s*, archaeologists discovered something that cleared up part of **ancient Egyptian** history – a *2,700*-year-old **city** hiding deep below the turquoise water of the *Mediterranean Sea.*

The city, *Thonis–Heracleion,* once stood on the coast of **Egypt.**

Traders from all over Europe sailed there to buy and sell everything from perfume to pottery.

Then, in the 8th Century CE – after many disastrous **earthquakes** and **floods** – Thonis-Heracleion was swallowed up by the sea. **Gulp.**

For over a *thousand years,* it lay **lost** beneath the waves . . .

... until *1933*, when a pilot flying over the Egyptian Coast spotted **curious shadows** lurking in the water. Was this the

LOST CITY?

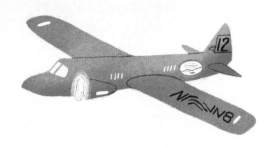

63 years later in *1996*, a team of international experts, led by the French underwater **archaeologist** *Franck Goddio*, began mapping the area from aboard their surveying boat, **Princess Duda**.

Four years later, divers finally swam down to begin digging . . .

To dig, *Franck's* team used giant underwater vacuum cleaners called **dredgers.**

They sucked up thick layers of sand and clay to reveal something truly **SAND-TASTIC** . . . a treasure trove of *ancient goodies.*

They found the ruins of magnificent *temples*, gigantic *stone statues* of Egyptian gods, *perfume bottles*, precious *jewelry, gold coins*, and much more.

Archaeologists are still discovering things **20 years later!** One thing's for sure . . . there are many more **as-THONIS-hing** stories to come!

We Dug Up an ARMY

Chinese farmers drilling for water in 1974 made a **MAJOR discovery** when they dug up the head of an *ancient pottery soldier* ... and then an **entire army** of nearly *8,000* life-sized model *warriors*.

The **underground army** had been secretly guarding the tomb of China's first emperor, *Qin Shi Huang di*, for over *2,200 years*, when it finally came to the world's **attention**.

To find out how the soldiers got there, we need to march back in time to *246 BCE*, when *Emperor Qin* came to power.

Although he was only **13 years old**, the emperor immediately began creating his own *magnificent burial ground* near the royal city of *Xianyang* (close to modern-day Xian).

The gigantic site was like an **underground kingdom**, containing everything he needed for the *afterlife*.

As part of the preparations, Emperor Qin ordered *700,000* craft workers to sculpt a **huge ARMY**, from a type of pottery called *terracotta*.

Incredibly, each soldier was *unique*, with different **clothes, faces** and **hairstyles!**

He believed the model warriors – equipped with *deadly weapons, horses,* and *chariots* – would keep him **safe** in the next world.

Once complete, the warriors were **painted** in bright colours, lined up **ready for battle** and buried in **deep pits!**

Archaeologists have found other pits nearby filled with terracotta models of **slaves, musicians, acrobats,** and even **muscly strongmen** designed to **serve** and **entertain** the emperor in the next world.

When Emperor Qin died, aged 38, he was buried in a huge tomb under a hill, not far from his warriors.

Ancient writings say that the tomb is filled with *priceless treasures.*

Some archaeologists believe it is surrounded by a river of *poisonous liquid metal,* called mercury.

Meanwhile, others think it is *booby-trapped* with crossbows that are set to fire if they are disturbed!

Whatever the truth, **nobody** is prepared to risk such **grave danger** and, to this day, no archaeologist has **dared** excavate the tomb!

We Dug Up the ROSETTA STONE

In 1799, invading French soldiers led by *Lieutenant Pierre François Xavier Bouchard* were repairing a fort near the Egyptian town of *el-Rashid (Rosetta)* when they made a discovery that would **ROCK the world.**

As Pierre watched his team dig, something ***unusual*** caught his attention . . .

It was a **HUGE** slab of **black stone with writing carved onto it.** The writing was in three languages: *ancient Greek*, everyday ancient Egyptian writing (*Egyptian Demotic*) and Egyptian *hieroglyphs.*

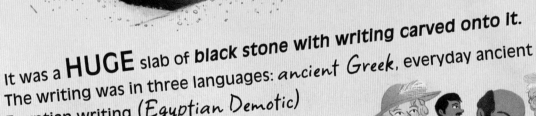

Curious to find out what it said, Pierre smuggled the rock out of Egypt to be ***examined by experts***, who discovered part of an official message written 2,000 years earlier by **powerful** *Egyptian Priests.*

Hieroglyphs are a form of writing that uses **symbols** instead of letters. **Egyptians** stopped using hieroglyphs around **400 CE** and, over time, everyone completely **forgot how to read them**. Although people had tried for many years, by the time of our story, the **code** had remained **secret for centuries!**

In it, the priests declared their support for Egypt's king – 13-year-old *Ptolemy the Fifth*. And they'd carved their message in three languages to make sure *everyone* could read it.

Centuries later, experts could use the Greek words on the stone to *decode the hieroglyphic symbols* carved above them.

It wasn't an easy code to crack . . .

. . . but, *twenty years later*, French scholar *Jean-François Champollion* finally worked it all out.

His brilliant breakthrough meant that historians could read and understand the many *HIEROGLYPHS* carved and painted onto the walls of ancient Egyptian *monuments, tombs, and temples.*

The *Rosetta Stone* was sent to the *British Museum* after Britain defeated Napoleon in 1801. Egyptian archaeologists are **campaigning** for it to be **returned to Egypt.**

It was a **momentous milestone** in the modern world's understanding of ancient Egypt.

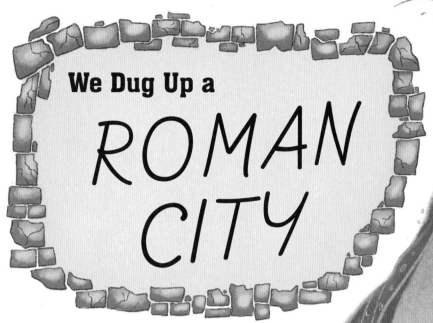

We Dug Up a ROMAN CITY

Nearly 2,000 years ago, in 79 *CE*, a **volcano** called *Mount Vesuvius* in **Italy** erupted. The hot ash, stones and poisonous gases completely buried the city of *Pompeii*. It remained hidden until *1594*, when an architect called *Domenico Fontana* stumbled across the ruins.

150 years later, experts started digging out the city and **unearthed** . . .

shops . . . fast food restaurants . . . theaters . . . public baths . . . temples . . .

. . . hundreds of homes with *beautifully painted walls* and *floor mosaics* . . .

and a **HUGE** *amphitheater* where **gladiators** fought to the death.

In **1863**, an archaeologist called **Giuseppe Fiorelli** found traces of the Pompeian people. Although the bodies had long since rotted away, they'd left **human-shaped holes** inside the hardened ash. By pouring **plaster** into the holes, Fiorelli created **models** of the people, which revealed how they died, what they were doing and even what sort of clothing they wore.

But there's **more!**

Hidden inside Pompeii's buildings, archaeologists have discovered **perfectly preserved** signs of everyday life . . .

from *bread loaves* in **bakers' ovens** . . .

and ornaments and coins . . .

. . . to *bowls* for *food* and *jewelry*. . . .

They've even found *graffiti on walls* showing **math calculations, insults,** and **love notes.**

So although *Vesuvius* destroyed POMPEII, it also **protected** and **preserved** it, allowing the modern world a peek at what life was like for ordinary *Romans* in the 1st century CE.

Today, *Pompeii's* streets are alive again with crowds of **curious tourists** who visit in their millions each year!

We Dug Up a SHIP

In the summer of 1939, archaeologists made *big waves* when they discovered something **peculiar** buried in the grounds of a country house called *Sutton Hoo* in *Suffolk*, UK.

The house belonged to *Edith Pretty* and her son *Robert*, and in the grounds surrounding it was a field with 18 **mysterious** mounds of earth.

Curious to find out what lay beneath, Edith hired an archaeologist called *Basil Brown* to start digging.

Basil soon found *iron weapons* and some *iron bolts* (rivets). Intrigued, and with the help of other archaeologists, such as *Peggy Piggott*, Basil kept digging.

And digging.

And digging.

Until he found something

Spectacular!

Beneath the sandy soil was the shape of an **enormous 88-feet-long** SHIP. The timbers had rotted away, leaving a ghostly imprint in the ground.

In the middle of the ship, Basil discovered an ancient burial chamber full of the most sparkling treasures.

There were *silver bowls* from Constantinople (now called Istanbul) . . .

gold buckles set with precious *gemstones* . . .

. . . a *sword* with a bejeweled handle . . .

. . . and a *helmet* decorated with a dragon.

To his amazement, Basil had unearthed the burial site of a powerful and wealthy 7th Century **Anglo-Saxon king** called *Raedwald*.

Although the treasure belonged to Edith, she gave it all to the *British Museum*.

For a long time, people believed that when the Romans left Britain, there were no **great leaders**, no **scientific achievements** and no **talented artists**. But the treasures Basil found at Sutton Hoo prove just how wrong they were.

We Dug Up the PLAGUE

Archaeologists made a **fang-tastically** gruesome discovery when they dug up some *700-year-old* **teeth** in *Kyrgyzstan* (in Central Asia).

Our story begins in the late *1340s* when a **deadly disease** – or *'plague'* – swept through Europe, Asia and North Africa, killing **tens of millions** of people.

The mysterious illness was nicknamed the *'Black Death'* after nasty **black blotches** that appeared on infected people's skin.

Back then, nobody understood where the plague had come from or how it spread. We now know that it was caused by *bacteria* (tiny living germs) called **Y pestis**.

Y pestis started life in the **blood** of small animals called **rodents** (most likely marmots or rats). At some point, **fleas** living on these rodents hopped onto **humans** for a bite to eat – **carrying and spreading the bacteria** with them.

Until recently, nobody knew exactly **where** in the world and **when** the Black Death began. All that changed when archaeologists began investigating a large group of *tombstones* by a lake in *Kyrgyzstan*.

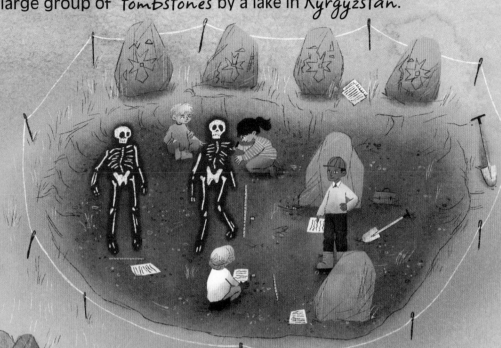

Writing on these stones revealed that the people buried beneath had all died of a *strange illness* between *1338* and *1339* – around ten years **before** the black death began its *ruthless rampage*.

Could these have been the **first ever human victims** of the

BLACK DEATH?

Convinced they were onto something, the archaeologists asked scientists to examine *teeth* from the buried bodies.

Teeth contain lots of **blood vessels** and plague-causing bacteria can **linger** in blood.

To their amazement the experts discovered traces of Y pestis in the gnarly old gnashers!

Although scientists need more evidence to be absolutely sure . . . they are confident that they've finally drilled down to the tooth of where and when history's **most deadly pandemic** began.

We Dug Up a
KING

When they die, **kings** and **queens** are usually laid to rest in *magnificent tombs*. So, spare a thought for *King Richard III* of England, who was found buried beneath . . . *a parking lot.*

Let's travel back in time to a marshy plain at *Bosworth Field* in the English county of *Leicestershire*. Here, on *August 22 1485*, a **battle for the throne** was raging between *Richard* and *Henry Tudor*.

Despite putting up an impressive fight, Richard was **killed** by a blow to the head. His rival was crowned *King Henry VII* and Richard's body was carted off for burial in a church in *Leicester*.

Years passed . . .

. . . the church was **demolished** and the royal grave was *lost* . . .

. . . until *2009*, when a historian called *Philippa Langley* studied some old maps and became **convinced** that the spot where the church once stood was now a **scruffy parking lot**.

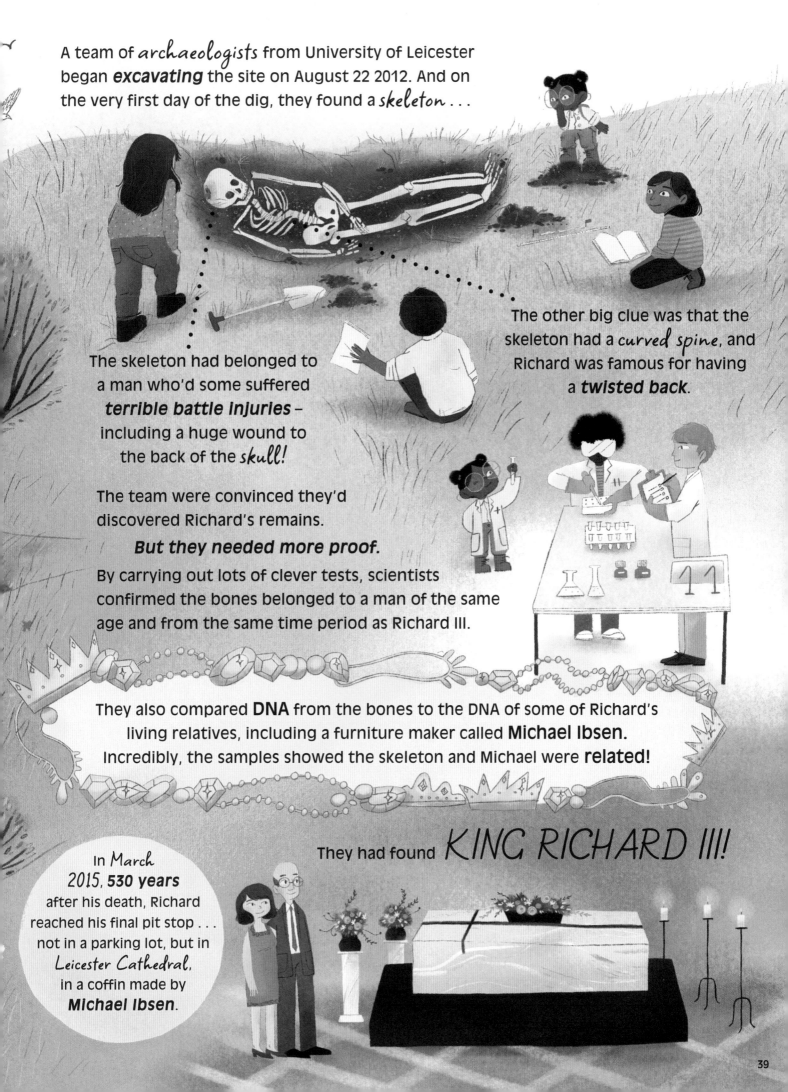

A team of **archaeologists** from University of Leicester began **excavating** the site on August 22 2012. And on the very first day of the dig, they found a *skeleton* . . .

The skeleton had belonged to a man who'd some suffered **terrible battle injuries** – including a huge wound to the back of the *skull!*

The team were convinced they'd discovered Richard's remains.
But they needed more proof.
By carrying out lots of clever tests, scientists confirmed the bones belonged to a man of the same age and from the same time period as Richard III.

The other big clue was that the skeleton had a *curved spine*, and Richard was famous for having a **twisted back**.

They also compared **DNA** from the bones to the DNA of some of Richard's living relatives, including a furniture maker called **Michael Ibsen**. Incredibly, the samples showed the skeleton and Michael were **related!**

In *March* **2015, 530 years** after his death, Richard reached his final pit stop . . . not in a parking lot, but in *Leicester Cathedral,* in a coffin made by **Michael Ibsen**.

They had found KING RICHARD III!

We Dug Up the
TITANIC

On *April 15 1912*, the world's **biggest** and most **luxurious ship**, the mighty *Titanic*, sunk to the bottom of the **Atlantic Ocean**, and was lost for *73 years*.

The Titanic set sail from *Southampton*, England to *America*, on her first ever voyage on *April 10 1912*.

However, shortly before midnight on April 14, the Titanic **hit an iceberg . . .** and **sank** in just over two and a half hours.

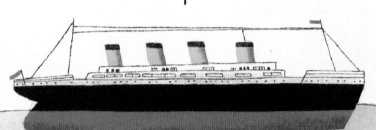

With far **too few** *lifeboats* for the 2,200 people on board, only around 705 survived.

Many people searched for the famous ship without luck. Finally, in *1985*, after weeks of careful searching with a **remote-controlled** *submarine*, a US and French expedition found her.

The contents of the ship lay *scattered* for **miles** around.

The ship had *broken* into two pieces, which were sitting on the ocean floor at a depth of *12,500 feet*. The wreck was so *deep* that nobody could scuba dive down to take a closer look.

However, in 1987, another team visited the site with a newly designed **French submarine** called the *Nautile*. It carried a crew of three people and had two **robotic arms.**

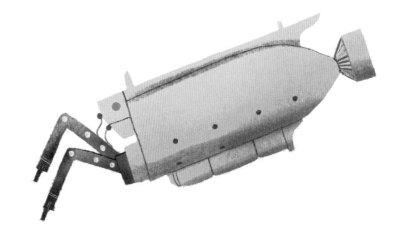

The crew used the arms to gather up hundreds of objects, including:

fine china dinner plates . . .

a *stained-glass* window . . .

chandeliers . . .

a *chamber pot* . . .

and a *suitcase* filled with *jewelry* and *money.*

Each one had been kept fresh by the cold and dark conditions on the seabed.

Since 1987, more than **5,000 artefacts** have been recovered from the wreck site, but many believe they should have been left at the bottom of the ocean, as a **mark of respect** to all the people who lost their lives on the

TITANIC.

One thing that will never be saved, though, is the **ship** itself. After more than **100 years** of being attacked by **salt water**, **iron-munching bacteria**, and **strong ocean currents**, some experts predict it will **disappear** completely within the next **30 years!**

LOST TREASURES

The diggers you've met in this book
found some *amazing* things.

But, of course, when it comes to
digging stuff up, humans have only
just **scratched the surface!**

There are **countless** more lost
'treasures' just waiting to be found!

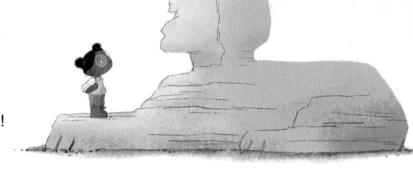

Some are so **well hidden** that people have
been searching for them for **centuries** . . .

Like the *2,000*-year-old **tomb** of Egypt's last pharaoh,
Queen Cleopatra VII, which lies somewhere
near the Egyptian city of *Alexandria* . . .

Or the wreck of the *Señor San Miguel* –
a Spanish **treasure ship** that sunk in a storm
off the coast of *Florida*, in the USA, in 1715.

Carrying *jewels, gold goblets, silver plates,
gold bullion,* and *coins,* it is thought to
be one of the **richest** treasure ships
ever to have been lost.

Then there are the buried **marvels** that people think
might exist . . . but no one can say for sure.

Like the site of the mysterious
Hanging Gardens of Babylon
– one of the **Seven Wonders**
of the Ancient World.

Archaeologists believe these fabulous
'tiered' gardens were built by a powerful
king or queen over 2,600 years ago in
the country we now call *Iraq*.

However, despite a lot of digging,
nobody knows exactly where!

Or . . .
King John of England's war chest,
a box bursting with **gold** and **jewels**.

The chest is said to have been sucked
into a sea of mud in 1216 as the
villainous king fled from an invading
French army over marshland.

Then, there are the 'wonders' that most people accept only existed in **legends** . . . but that some very hopeful people search for anyway!

Like the . . .

Lost City of Atlantis:

a rich and powerful island kingdom that is said to have **sunk** into the depths of the Atlantic Ocean 9,000 years ago.

And the fabled

City of Gold - El Dorado -

which explorers have searched for amongst the **mountains** and **jungles** of South America for centuries.

Finally, of course, there are **spadefuls** of things that we don't even realise have been lost from . . .

ancient shards of *pottery* to 'new' species of *dinosaurs* . . .
all lying there just waiting to be dug up by some lucky person!

And who knows? That someone could **well** be *YOU!*

GLOSSARY

Afterlife: Where ancient Egyptians believed they would go after they died.

Amphitheater: A circular or oval-shaped open-air theater.

Anthropology: The study of human beings, from prehistoric times to today.

Archaeology: The study of the past through the things that people made, used, and left behind.

Artefact: An object that has been made by humans.

Asteroid: A rocky object that orbits (goes around) the Sun.

Bacteria: Tiny, simple living things that can only be seen through a microscope.

Blood Vessels: Small tubes that carry blood around our bodies.

Booby trap: A hidden or disguised contraption designed to surprise or harm someone.

Comet: An object made of dust and ice that orbits (goes around) the Sun.

Con artist: Someone who cheats or tricks others by making them believe something that is not true.

Coprolite: Poo that has been fossilized (turned into a fossil).

Crater: A large bowl-shaped hole in the ground that has been caused by a meteorite, volcanic activity, or an explosion.

Creek: A stream or narrow river.

Demotic language: Language used by ordinary everyday people.

Demolished: Pulled or knocked down.

DNA: The material (stuff) inside living things that carries all the instructions for how they grow, look, and work. Living things inherit (get) DNA from their parents.

Excavate: To dig a hole or to uncover and remove something from the ground.

Extinction: The dying out of a species.

Fossils: The remains or traces of plants and animals that lived a long time ago.

Glacier: A slow-moving river of ice.

Hieroglyphs: A way of writing that uses pictures and symbols instead of letters and words.

Ice Age: A period when the climate was much colder than it is today and most of the Earth's surface was buried under sheets of ice.

Iridium: A hard silvery metal that is extremely rare on Earth, but is often found in asteroids.

Jurassic: A period in history, 199 million to 145 million years ago, when dinosaurs roamed the Earth.

Meteorite: A piece of rock or metal that has fallen to the Earth's surface from outer space.

Minerologist: Someone who studies minerals.

Minerals: Solid substances that occur naturally and that make up the Earth's rocks, sands, and soils. Salt, iron and diamond are all examples of minerals.

Momentous: Really important.

Monument: A statue, building, or other structure that celebrates or marks an important person or event.

Mosaic: A picture made by arranging small pieces of stone, tile, or glass.

Mummified: A dead body that has been preserved (prevented from rotting) by being dried or using a special process called embalming.

Neanderthals: An extinct species of human that lived from about 400,000 to 40,000 years ago.

Palaeontology: The study of fossilized animals and plants.

Palaeontologist: Someone who studies fossils to find out about the history of life on Earth.

Plague: An infectious disease that spreads quickly, killing large numbers of people.

Prehistoric: Something that happened in the period of history before humans had learned to write.

Reptile: An animal (for example, a snake, lizard, turtle, or alligator) that has cold blood, that lays eggs and that has a body covered with scales.

Rodents: Mammals with long and sharp front teeth used for gnawing. Rats, mice, squirrels, chipmunks, gerbils, hamsters, guinea pigs, and porcupines are all rodents.

Sacred: Holy; something that is connected with a god.

Shrine: A case or box containing sacred remains or objects.

Species: A group of living things that are similar to each other. Humans, dogs, and sunflowers are all examples of species.

Stone Age: A period of prehistory when humans used stone tools. It lasted around 2.5 million years and ended around 5,000 years ago when humans began making tools and weapons from a metal called bronze.

Tiered: A series of rows placed one above the other – like seating in a theater or sports stadium.

Tomb: A stone building or underground room where someone is buried.

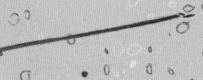

To Ally, Hugh and William – the most faithful and
fun digging companions a cousin could wish for ~ A S

For Mum and Dad ~ K H

LAURENCE KING
First published in the United States in 2023 by
Laurence King

ISBN: 9781510230415

10 9 8 7 6 5 4 3 2 1

Printed in China

MIX
Paper from
responsible sources
FSC
www.fsc.org   FSC® C104740

Laurence King
An imprint of
Hachette Children's Group
Part of Hodder and Stoughton
Carmelite House
50 Victoria Embankment
London EC4Y 0DZ

An Hachette UK Company
www.hachette.co.uk
www.hachettechildrens.co.uk
www.laurenceking.com